Hafnwiler Danckes Beunt Berget

waldorf Wintrbach wil. Schuß Weingartn Zankel Kißle

kenburen Pafendorf Ravespurg

Sikingen Cell Augia minor Luipolds

Bermatin Heppach Guler Walt

gen Tal dor. Eschach Waldburg

Markdorf Brochn Pfrrich Pratsberg

urg cell Rat

Hagnow Mekanbeurn Wangen

Fischb ac Mancell Haslach Hidenfwilr

Buchorn Erßkirch Fe Autnang Z Asschen

Zoll Achberg Sirgen

DENSEE Langnaw Rogncel Hofenb

Langen Argen Waßer Herknswiler Ruksteig

burg Reuti Herbrands L

Alwin Bucburg Tobel

Bregentz Hirsberg

Lindaw Pfanenberg Cs

Rhenus flu. Angia Major

hell Mecheraw Bregentz

Arbon Ror Ach

fen Rosschach Hochst Fulsach Wolfurt

b. Stai nach

August 2005

Dear Cathryn,

Dear Greg,

Dear Matt,

As a memory of your trip to south Germany
and a very warm invitation to return some time!

It was a great pleasure to have you here!

Yours Steve

Stephan Bissinger

Doebeleshasse 40
D-78 462 Konstanz

T: 0049-7531-368516

Schafberjweg 68
D-74376 Gemmrigheim

0049-7143-94783

A Look at
Lake Constance

Rolf Zimmermann

Stadler Verlagsgesellschaft mbH

Lake Constance (in German: Bodensee)

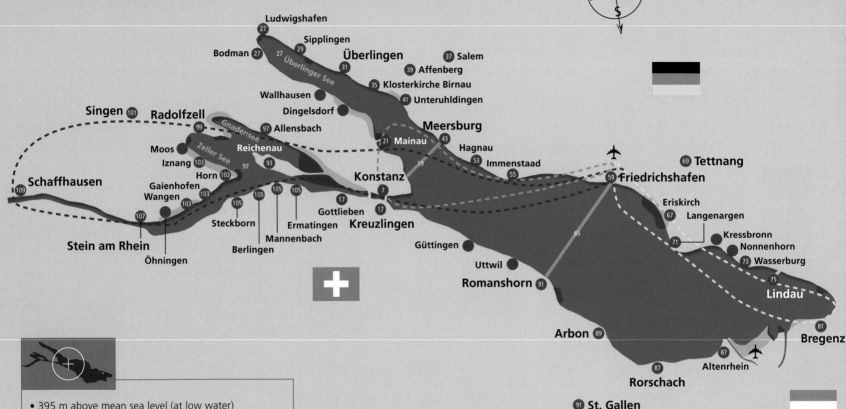

- 395 m above mean sea level (at low water)
- 63 km long (Bregenz – Ludwigshafen)
- Up to 14 km wide
- Greatest depth 252 m, average depth 96 m (at low water)
- 520 to 580 km² surface area, depending on water level
- 50 to 52 billion m³ volume, depending on water level
- Water balance per average year: inflow 12 billion m³, evaporation 0.3 billion m³, extraction for drinking water 0.18 billion m³
- Biggest tributaries: Rhine (Rhein), Bregenzer Ach, Argen, Radolfzeller Aach, Schussen
- Biggest cities: Constance (Konstanz), Friedrichshafen, Radolfzell, Bregenz, Lindau, Überlingen

——	Route car ferries
——	The most important nature reserves
——	Closed water areas
– – –	Zeppelin western route
········	Zeppelin eastern route
– – – –	Zeppelin route Rhine Falls/Schaffhausen
⑦	Place (with page number)

Lake Constance belongs to the Rhine river system and has a catchment area of about 11,500 km². It contains substantially more water than the rest of the Rhine and supplies over four million people with drinking water.

Contents

Lake Constance and its Names

S everal finds from the Stone Age and Bronze Age prove that the area around Lake Constance has been populated for about ten thousand years.

More than 2000 years ago the Romans conquered a small settlement on the eastern border of the lake and expanded it to form a trade and military base, which they named Brigantium. This base later became what nowadays is known as Bregenz. The Romans named the lake "Lacus Brigantinus".

Around the year 260 the Alemannians invaded the northern areas around the lake. In order to secure the northern border of the Roman Empire, an existing base on the western outflow was upgraded to a fort. This was done under the reign of the emperor Constantius Chlorus around the year 300 A.D. The fort was named Constantia and from this the city Constance (Konstanz) evolved, after which the lake is named in most foreign languages, e.g. "Lake Constance" and "Lac de Constance".

In the twelfth century the Staufer named the lake after their imperial palace Bodama, which is the present day Bodman by the Lower Lake (Untersee). This is how the names "Lacus Bodamicus", "Bodamer See", and finally the present day name "Bodensee" came into being.

We will now go on a tour around the lake and get to know its landscapes and towns, its churches, and other worthwhile sights.

"Lacus Bodamicus" on a map from the year 1702

p.4: Only once we see Lake Constance from the air do we get an impression of its immense size, here an extract with Überlinger See

Constance (Konstanz)

We will start our tour in Constance, the largest and most well-known city by Lake Constance. Due to its favorable location on several trade routes, Constance, which used to be a Roman settlement, became a bishop's seat in the year 590. Old Constance was a fortified city on the left bank of the Rhine, however, already in the Middle Ages a wooden bridge was built to what nowadays is the district of Petershausen on the right bank of the Rhine.

Seeing as the Swiss city of Kreuzlingen borders Constance to the south, the city expanded to the north with new suburbs being built on the right bank of the Rhine. Several bridges connect the different parts of Constance.

* Largest city on Lake Constance
* Free city of the Empire during the Middle Ages and location of the Council 1414 – 1418
* Approximately 80,000 inhabitants
* University town with 12,000 students
* Theater and philharmonic concert hall
* Most famous landmarks: the Minster and the Council Building
* Archaeological Regional Museum, Rosgarten Museum, Aquarium "Sea Life", Lake Constance Nature Museum, and many more
* Various recreational facilities
* Annual "Seenachtsfest" in cooperation with Kreuzlingen

Bottom: The Insel Hotel, a former Dominican monastery next to the city park

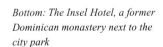

Top: Bridge across the Rhine with a view of the minster and the Rheintorturm

Middle: Art Nouveau houses in the Seestraße

p.6: In Constance the Upper Lake leads into the Lake Rhine, which is crossed by many bridges

Constance

Council Building and Harbor

In order to get to the banks of Lake Constance from the old town we have to cross the busy "Konzilstraße" and the railroad tracks. One building right by the harbor cannot be overlooked. This is the so-called Council Building. It was built in 1388 as a warehouse and depot for trade with Southern Europe and as a site for the "Konstanzer Leinwandmesse" (linen trade fair). Just a few years later it made history for four days.

The most significant gathering of the Late Middle Ages took place in Constance between 1414 and 1418: the "Council of Constance". This is where the church, which was divided at the time, was reformed. This is also where one pope was elected to replace the three existing popes and antipopes. The council usually met in the minster, but for the election 56 cardinals and envoys locked themselves in the first floor of the Council Building for a conclave between November 8 and 11, 1417 and elected the Roman Oddone Colonna to become Pope Martin V.

At the time Constance had only 6,000 inhabitants and during the conclave the city had to accommodate up to 30,000 foreigners at the same time. Among these were about 200 bakers, barbers, and tailors each, as well as 700 courtesans called "Hübschlerinnen". In reference to this the Bodmanian artist Peter Lenk created the sparsely clad sculpture "Imperia", which measures nine meters in height and weighs eighteen tons. Since 1993 she has been turning around her own axis at the entrance to the harbor and has become another landmark of Constance. She is holding Emperor Sigismund and Pope Martin V. on her hands and so symbolizes the power of the courtesans during the Council.

Top left: The Council Building nowadays houses a restaurant and conference facilities

Middle: The Imperia awaits at the harbor entrance

Top right: Boats by Constance

p.8: Picture of the Imperia, harbor, and Zeppelin monument taken against the light

Constance

In the Old Town

From here we take the pedestrian underpass, which leads us to the "Marktstätte", a somewhat oblong town square surrounded by houses that represent the past eight centuries. Seeing as Constance is so close to Switzerland, it was not bombed during the Second World War. Therefore, there are still many buildings, here and in other parts of

the old town, that bear witness to the great past between the thirteenth and sixteenth century. Constance was a free city of the Empire with self-confident merchants and citizens. The city had the right to mint coins as well as the right to levy import duties. Linen from Constance was a well-known article for European trading.

The old fortifications have disappeared and only the "Schnetztor" on the southwestern corner of the old town as well as the "Pulverturm" and the "Rheintorturm" in the north by the Lake Rhine remain.

The historic "Altstadt" or old town is bordered to the west by a well shaded avenue, the upper and lower parts of

which are called the "Obere -" and "Untere Laube" respectively. In 1990 a triumphal arch was built on its median strip, the "Konstanzer Triumphbogen", with which the artist Peter Lenk caricatures our society, in particular our obsession with cars and the way we spend our leisure time.

Top left: The city hall is the former guild house of the linen weavers of the sixteenth century

Top right: The only preserved city gate is the Schnetztor in the southwest of the old town

Bottom: The Lenk Fountain on the Untere Laube caricatures the car mania of our society

p.10: The Marktstätte in the center of the old town

11

Constance

The Minster

The minster square is situated at the highest point of the old town. In the year 1052 the bishop's church collapsed and subsequently construction began on the Romanesque Minster "Unsere Liebe Frau zu Konstanz" which means "Our Dear Lady of Constance". In the course of the following centuries it underwent several changes through the addition of Gothic and Baroque parts. Among one of these additions is the neo-Gothic top of the tower, which was added during the nineteenth century. With its height of 76 meters it literally towers above the rooftops of the old town of Constance.

For a long time Constance was the largest diocese in Germany and the minster was an important place of pilgrimage on one of the pilgrim's routes to Santiago de Compostela. Unfortunately, we can only visit very few of the numerous Middle Age church treasures as most of them were destroyed during the Reformation under Ulrich Zwingli.

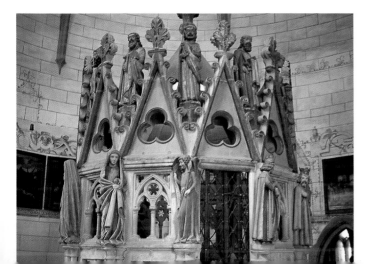

Top: View of the Renaissance organ of the minster

Bottom left: The Mauritius Rotunda, during the Middle Ages an important stop on the Schwabenweg pilgrimage path to Santiago de Compostela

Bottom right: One of the four Gold Discs of Constance in the crypt of the minster

p.12: New Gothic tower of the minster and the Mariensäule from the year 1693

Constance

University and FH Konstanz

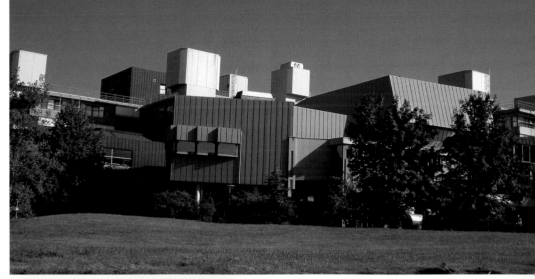

In 1964 the federal parliament of Baden-Württemberg decided to establish a so-called reform university. In theory such a university would offer lectures in small groups, students would receive intensive guidance by tutors and would take part in research work done by professors. The

University of Constance
* Established in 1966 as a reform university
* 13 departments and 41 study courses with a focus on natural sciences, humanities, and administrative sciences
* 8,500 students

FH Konstanz
* University of Applied Sciences for technology, commerce, and design
* 23 study courses
* 3,500 students

idea became reality when lectures started in the fall of 1966 with 7 professors and 57 students. They were held in the "Inselhotel" on a provisional basis.

Today the actual number of students far exceeds the initially planned maximum of 3,000. There are approximately 8,500 students on the "Campus auf dem Gießberg". Paths were kept short in the complex of buildings

above Überlinger See. Furthermore, by using different architectural styles and a lot of "Art on the Construction Site" a barren landscape of concrete blocks was avoided.

The FH Konstanz University of Applied Sciences is significantly older than the university. It originated from the "Technikum Konstanz" (technical college), which took up its lectures in 1906 with 4 lecturers and 28 students.

Top and middle left: Buildings of different styles and colors are interconnected

Middle right: Central forum of the FH Konstanz

p.14: One of the many spots for breaks between lectures

Kreuzlingen and Gottlieben

Shopping street in Kreuzlingen decorated with flags

Before we leave Constance in the direction of Überlinger See we are going to have a look at these two Swiss neighbors.

During the nineteenth century Kreuzlingen was still a tiny village with a history which was closely connected to that of Constance. It was only in 1928 that the present day city came into being when several neighboring municipalities were joined together. The former convent St. Ulrich together with its "Ölbergkapelle" to the east and the convent's summer residence, Seeburg, on the banks of the lake were part of this amalgamation. The "Kornschütte" in the Seeburgpark houses the Lake Museum with expositions on navigation and fishing on Lake Constance.

To the west of Kreuzlingen at the end of the Lake Rhine lies Gottlieben, which is one of the smallest communities in Switzerland. The castle from the thirteenth century, which now belongs to the singer Lisa Della Casa and her family, is hidden behind several tall trees. Three renowned gourmet restaurants are definitely less hidden in their picturesque half-timbered houses. Not only do they offer a good meal but also a beautiful view of the Lake Rhine and the Wollmating Reed, which lies on the opposite side.

Kreuzlingen

* Swiss sister city of Constance
* Approximately 18,000 inhabitants
* Lake Museum on navigation and fishing history, Puppet Museum and several more museums
* Theater, concert hall, planetarium
* Ice rink, swimming pools etc.
* Annual "Seenachtsfest" in cooperation with Constance

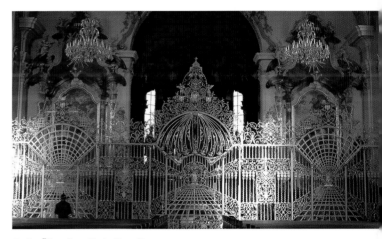

In the Ölbergkapelle in Kreuzlingen

Bottom left: From the shipping pier one has a view across the Lake Rhine to the Wollmating Reed

Bottom right: The Drachenburg in Gottlieben is one of the most famous gourmet restaurants in the region

p.16: The Seeburg was the summer residence of the monastery St. Ulrich and nowadays is a restaurant

The "Swimming Bridge"
Constance – Meersburg

Now back to the German banks of Lake Constance. To the north of Constance the Upper Lake (Obersee), which is up to 14 kilometers wide, narrows to about three to four kilometers where it changes its name to Überlinger See. Already during Roman times ships were crossing Lake Constance here. During the 1920s the increase in motor traffic and the isolated location of the border town Constance raised the issue of finding a way to cross Überlinger See with a ferry that could transport motor vehicles. On September 30, 1928 the first ferry, named "Konstanz", made the trip between Konstanz-Staad and Meersburg. The "Konstanz" was 32 meters long and could transport a maximum of 15 cars and 200 people.

Nowadays, up to six significantly larger ferries connect the cities of Constance and Meersburg as a "swimming bridge" at any time of day and night.

At night the ferries only travel on an hourly basis, whereas during the day they travel every ten minutes during peak hours. In so doing, the ferries transport more than two million cars, utility vehicles, motorcycles, and bicycles and more than five million people every year.

Top left: Design of the new ferry

Top right: Ferry on entering the ferry harbor in Konstanz-Staad

Bottom: Night-time ambience on the ferry

p.18: Modern ferries transport up to 68 cars and up to 700 people across the lake in 15 minutes

Flower Isle Mainau

O ur "round trip" around Lake Constance takes us along Überlinger See. Just a few kilometers behind Konstanz-Staad we reach Mainau Island. This Flower Isle also has a turbulent history. For several centuries it was in the possession of the Abbey of Reichenau, which, along with some other neighboring villages, donated it to the Knights of the Teutonic Order in the year 1272. Due to the secularization, Mainau Island fell

Mainau
* One of the most beautiful parks in the world
* Trees of close to 150 years of age with more than 500 different types of deciduous and coniferous trees
* Since 1888 a collection of palms
* Since 1996 a butterfly house with 25 colorful species
* Many events and open-air festivals
* Own harbor
* Open year-round, 1.5 million visitors annually

into the possession of the House of Baden at the beginning of the nineteenth century. Grand Duke Friedrich I. bought the island in 1853 and used it as a summer residence from the year 1857 onward. He had the park planted with several majestic trees and the first rose gardens. He also had greenhouses set up, filled with exotic plants.

After his death in 1907 the park fell into decay until his great grandson from the Swedish line of descent, Count Lennart Bernadotte, inherited the island in 1930. It was only under his supervision that Mainau Island became today's Flower Isle.

Top: View of the palace and the palm house behind, which is only taken down during summer

Bottom: In the Baroque palace church

p.20: The Baroque palace from the eighteenth century towers above the rose gardens

Flower Isle Mainau

Flowers Throughout the Year

T he parks and gardens of Mainau Island are open year-round. Whoever does not arrive by boat at the harbor, can take a bridge from the parking lot to the island and in so doing passes by the so-called "Schwedenkreuz" (Cross of the Swedes). Apparently this bronze crucifixion group was stolen from the island by Swedish mercenaries during the Thirty Years' War, but due to its weight they threw it into the lake at the spot where it stands today.

Mainau Island has flowers year-round. The first outdoor highlights of the park are thousands of tulips, hyacinths, and narcissi in the "Spring Avenue". From the end of May we can admire not only the 300,000 summer flowers but also the splendor of 30,000 roses in the "Italian Rose Garden" and by the promenade of wild roses. The highlight of the fall is the spectacle of dahlias with about 12,000 plants.

Top left: In spring – the tulip blossom

Top right: The event of the fall – the dahlia blossom

Left: Italian floral and water cascade in summer

Right: The so-called Schwedenkreuz

p.22: Again and again one looks across the flowerbeds toward the lake

23

Orchids
and Butterflies

During the winter season oranges and other citrus fruit as well as hundreds of orchids flower in the shelter of the palm houses next to the palace. However, even during the summer months we can find particularly beautiful orchids flowering among abundant tropical plants in the butterfly house, which was opened in 1996.

In this, the largest butterfly house in Germany, we can admire about 25 types of colorful butterflies from up close and follow their flight from blossom to blossom.

Top: Orchids flower year-round in the butterfly house

p.24 and bottom: Colorful butterflies fly from flower to flower

Überlinger See

To the northwest of Mainau Island, Überlinger See narrows to a width of about two kilometers. The lake is bordered by mountain ranges with steep banks on both sides, almost like a fjord. To the southwest the range is called the Bodanrück, to the northeast Sipplinger Berg, both of which are about 300 meters higher than the level of the lake.

A popular destination for excursions on the southwestern side of Überlinger See is the Marienschlucht (St. Mary's Gorge). A steep path along a little stream leads down to the lake across wooden steps.

The last villages at the northwestern end of Überlinger See are Bodman and on the northern bank Ludwigshafen. The former, at the time the imperial palace Bodama, gave the "Bodensee" and the "Bodanrück" their names.

Ludwigshafen came under Baden rule at the beginning of the nineteenth century. In 1826 an important freight and customs harbor was built under the order of Grand Duke Ludwig, who also gave the village its name.

Top: View of Überlinger See from Überlingen

Bottom left: In St. Mary's Gorge

Bottom right: Bodman Palace

p.26: View from Bodman to Ludwigshafen

Sipplingen

The village, which used to be a winegrowing and fishing village, lies on the steep slopes of the Sipplinger Berg, so that the lake is visible from almost every house. Nowadays, Sipplingen is a popular holiday destination with boat harbors and the theme center "Erlebniswelt Sipplingen", which has one of the largest model railway, model car, and toy collections. The former reptile zoo

of Unteruhldingen has been moved and is now part of the theme center.

Close to the village, water from the lake is taken from a depth of 60 meters and pumped up to the top of Sipplinger Berg, which lies at 700 meters above sea level. The water is then filtered in the water treatment plant of the "Bodensee Wasserversorgung" and is then pumped in enormous pipes in the direction of Stuttgart, where it supplies almost four million people in 320 cities and communities with drinking water.

On the slopes of the Sipplinger Berg lies the Haldenhof, a resort restaurant with a marvelous view and which is also the starting point of a geological trail.

Top left: View of Sipplingen from the Bodanrück

Top right: View of Sipplingen from the Haldenhof

Left: Steep molasse rocks by Goldbach have caves and tunnels

Middle: Water treatment plant

Right: Entrance of the theme center Erlebniswelt Sipplingen

p.28: Sipplingen

Überlingen

In the year 1191 Überlingen was granted a city charter by Emperor Friedrich I. Barbarossa and became a free city of the Empire a few years later. It was a trading center for corn, salt, and wine, a fact which made Überlingen a very prosperous city during the Middle Ages. As the city was not destroyed during the Thirty Years' War, several structures from this age remained intact, such as churches and the city hall as well as towers, gates, and trading and patrician houses.

During the nineteenth century the city became a popular health resort thanks to its protected southern exposure and its mineral springs, which were known since the Middle Ages. It only rains half as much here as it does in Bregenz. This is why there is an abundance of plants along the lake promenade. In the middle of the promenade, directly below the minster, lie the former granary "Greth" (nowadays a market hall) and the berth, both of which are popular meeting places for young and old.

* Health resort with "Lake Constance Thermal Bath", several health clinics, and sanatoria
* Former free city of the Empire, until 1972 district town
* Approximately 21,000 inhabitants
* Late Gothic minster with an unlike pair of towers
* Several museums
* A boardwalk of almost 4 km on the sunny "Riviera of Lake Constance"
* City park with cacti and other exotic plants
* Numerous recreational facilities

Top: Aerial photograph at sunset

Middle and bottom: Fountain by the berth with the author Martin Walser "on his high horse"

p.30: The berth below the minster is the center of the city

Überlingen

Minster St. Nicholas and the City Hall

St. Nicholas is the patron saint for not only children but also for fishermen, sailors, and merchants. This is why the fishermen and sailors of Überlingen named the minster after their patron saint. Construction was started in the year 1350. The northern church tower, which almost looks like a lighthouse, was expanded during the fifteenth and sixteenth century to its current height of 78 meters. The smaller southern tower has remained unchanged since 1444.

The minster is the largest Late Gothic church by Lake Constance. It became famous through the four-story high filigree-carved high altar that was created by Jörg Zürn between 1613 and 1616. To get a better view one can light it up for a few minutes by inserting a coin.

The city hall also dates back to the fourteenth and fifteenth century. Its greatest treasure is the wooden paneled council hall with its carved figures, which was created by Jakob Ruess between 1492 and 1494. The figures represent the classes of the German Empire.

p.32: The view from the garden of the Museum of Local History shows that the minster also has a more modest southern tower, apart from the immense northern tower

Top: Monument of Karl V. in front of the city hall

Middle left: High altar

Middle right: Coat of arms of the German Empire and the city of Überlingen in the council chamber

Birnau Pilgrimage Church

O ne of the landmarks of western Lake Constance is the Baroque pilgrimage church of Birnau. Situated amid vineyards, the abbey is visible from far away. The wide southern front with the tower faces the lake.

The late Baroque church with its provost building was built between 1746 and 1750 under the order of the Abbey of Salem. It served as a pilgrimage church and a summer residence for the abbots. The architect was Peter Thumb of Vorarlberg. Two more Austrians, the sculptor and stucco worker Josef Anton Feuchtmayer and the fresco painter Gottfried Bernhard Göz

crafted the interior of the church, which is flooded with light.

Birnau is most well-known for its numerous cherubs, especially the so-called Honeylicker (Honigschlecker) in front of the altar of St. Bernard. During the twelfth century Bernhard of Clairvaux was responsible for much of the expansion of the Cistercian Order, to which the Abbey of Salem also belonged. He was the most famous preacher of the Middle Ages and the Honeylicker is reminiscent of his often quoted "honey sweet eloquence".

Top left: The southern façade which includes the provost building

Top right: Visible from far away, the tower of the Birnau Pilgrimage Church is situated amid vineyards

Right: The Honeylicker

p.34: Baroque splendor of the nave, flooded with light

Salem Palace

The Abbey of Salem was founded in 1134 under the name of "Salomonsweiler". As it was a self-governing abbey of the Empire, it was the most important Cistercian monastery in Southern Germany for a long time. As a consequence of the secularization, it fell into the possession of the Margrave of Baden in 1802, who used it as a palace.

Since 1920 the west wing accommodates the famous boarding school Schloss Salem, which has two branches by Überlingen: Burg Hohenfels (lower school) and the newly constructed Salem International College.

Other parts of the palace are open to the public, including the library, emperor's hall, prelate's hall, and the Gothic minster. Another highlight is the fire-brigade museum, which was founded in 1976. Due to a devastating fire in 1697, the monks set up an exemplary fire watch more than 300 years ago, which today forms the basis of the museum. One can also visit an information center, the museum shop, and several arts and crafts workshops.

p.36 and top: Salem Palace

Bottom: Emperor's Hall

By the Affenberg

The "Prälatenweg" (prelate's path) passes between the Birnau church and the former Abbey of Salem. At approximately the halfway mark lies "Mendlishauser Hof", a former farm manor of the monastery. In 1976 twenty hectares of forest were fenced and colonized with a type of monkey called the Barbary Macaque. They originate from Morocco, where they live at altitudes of up to 2000 meters. As a consequence they are well suited to life in the open during the Lake Constance winter.

More than 200 of these trusting monkeys move freely among the visitors. We can observe the animals from up close and feed them specially prepared popcorn, which is available free of charge, while strolling along a 600 meter long circular path. This immediate contact without bars or ditches is a lot of fun, not only for the children. For us adults it is an experience as well to see the care of the mother animals for their young, the rollicking of the young monkeys, and the general social interaction of our animal relatives in a natural environment.

Apart from this, there are about 50 free-flying white storks that live on Mendlishauser Hof during the summer.

Top right: Young storks in the nest

p.38: Mendlishauser farmstead with the storks' nests

Unteruhldingen Pile Dwelling Museum

Top: The platforms and walk-ways were all built without the use of metal nails

Left: Deceptively real-looking figures bring the village to life

p.40: Pile Dwelling Museum of Unteruhldingen

* Museum since 1922
* 20 originally arranged reconstructions of pile dwellings of the Lake Constance region
* Stone Age village "Sipplingen" (3500 B.C.)
* Bronze Age village "Bad Buchau" (1050 B.C.)
* Bronze Age village "Unteruhldingen" (970 B.C.)
* About 300,000 visitors annually

The Pile Dwelling Museum displays reconstructions of settlements from the New Stone Age about 5,500 years ago and the Bronze Age about 3,000 years ago. The first two Stone Age house reconstructions were built in 1922 based on finds from excavations by Lake Constance and the Federsee. During the following years a village from the Bronze Age was constructed based on the example of the pile dwelling near the moated castle of Buchau.

Between 1999 and 2002 five more Late Bronze Age pile dwellings were added, constructed according to the most recent findings from the excavations at Unteruhldingen-Stollenwiesen. Within the framework of this project, which was supported by the European Union, the Swiss artist Gerry Embleton has complemented three of these houses with 27 human and animal figures. This is why we feel transported back to the everyday life of the Late Bronze Age 3,000 years ago.

Meersburg

For many people Meersburg is the most typical town on Lake Constance and the Old Castle is arguably the most well-known landmark in the Lake Constance region. This medieval castle, as well as the New Baroque Palace, was built on a natural terrace amid steep vineyards.

The Lower City with its picturesque half-timbered houses was established in the 13th century and has since grown on the embankments of the lake. The bank strip was widened repeatedly. The largest building there is the "Grethaus" which lies right by the port. It has a stepped gable and was previously used as a warehouse. Further to the east lie a harbor for pedal boats, a miniature golf course, and the new Meersburg Thermal Bath.

* A picturesque location for holidays or excursions
* Approximately 5,500 inhabitants
* The oldest inhabited castle in Germany
* New Palace with picture gallery and the Dornier Museum, international concerts in the palace
* Droste Museum in the "Fürstenhäusle", Bible Gallery, Zeppelin Museum, and many more museums
* Meersburg Thermal Bath and other recreational facilities
* Ferry to Constance and transfer point of the White Fleet

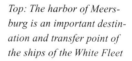

Top: The harbor of Meersburg is an important destination and transfer point of the ships of the White Fleet

Middle: Ship in front of the harbor entrance

Bottom: Outdoor pool of the new Meersburg Thermal Bath

p.42: High above the lake and above the Lower City lie the Old Castle, the New Palace, and the Upper City of Meersburg

43

Meersburg

The Old Castle

King Dagobert I. of the Merovingians, after whom the massive middle tower is named, supposedly initiated the construction of the Old Castle in the year 628. Subsequently, the Carolingians expanded the castle and used it as an imperial palace. The castle was never conquered and in 1268 it came into the possession of the prince bishops of Constance. Due to the Reformation, the bishop of the time had to leave Constance in the year 1526. He made his primary residence what was up until then his summer residence.

After the secularization, in 1838, the brother-in-law of the poetess Annette von Droste-Hülshoff bought the castle. Right up to the present day the castle is still inhabited by its private owners, but we can visit most of it. This means more than thirty furnished rooms, including a chapel, a knight's hall, a kitchen, and a dungeon. We can also visit the living area of Annette von Droste-Hülshoff, where she lived from 1841 to 1848, and the room in which she passed away. One of the Baroque halls nowadays accommodates a café with a roof garden, which offers one of the most beautiful views of the Lower City and the lake.

Top: View from the garden of the New Palace to the Old Castle

Bottom left: In the armory of the Old Castle

Bottom middle: Monument to the poetess Annette von Droste-Hülshoff

p. 44: The never-conquered Old Castle with the mighty Dagobert Tower

Meersburg

The New Palace

The prince bishops of Constance stayed in Meersburg, even after Constance became Catholic again in 1548. In 1712 the lengthy construction of the New Palace began and it finally served as a more feudal residence for the bishops from 1750 onwards.

The staircase of this Baroque palace was completed according to the designs of Balthasar Neumann. Nowadays, the representative halls of the palace provide space for the civic picture gallery, the Dornier Museum, several alternating exhibitions, and for festive events.

From the inner halls and from the garden on the side facing the lake we can see the Lower City and Lake Constance. Markets and wine festivals take place on the palace square on the northern side.

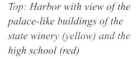

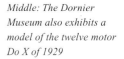

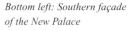

Top: Harbor with view of the palace-like buildings of the state winery (yellow) and the high school (red)

Middle: The Dornier Museum also exhibits a model of the twelve motor Do X of 1929

Bottom left: Southern façade of the New Palace

Bottom right: During the annual wine festival the Knabenmusik in historical costumes also comes to the fore

p.46: The Baroque New Palace was the residence of the prince bishops from 1750 to 1802

Meersburg

In the Old Town

The old town invites us for a stroll. Through every gate and behind every corner we find a new view of idyllic fountains and half-timbered houses, of painted gables and richly decorated oriels. Many of these old middle-class houses have been turned into hotels or restaurants. It is only the pulley beams above certain attic windows that reveal that the goods of merchants used to be stored there.

Two paths link the Upper Town and Lower Town. One can either take the steep steps along the walls of the Old Castle or one can take the lively street called "Steigstraße", which has many restaurants and souvenir shops.

Top left: On the Steigstraße

Top right: The Unterstadt-straße is an inviting place to stroll

Bottom: Historic watermill

p.48: The Hotel zum Bären and the Obertor

Viticulture by Lake Constance

It is not certain whether the Romans were the first to bring vines to Lake Constance. Nevertheless, winegrowing has been practiced at Lake Constance since the seventh century. Due to the altitude of the lake the vines need sunny slopes with a southern exposure. Most of these are to be found on the Baden banks between Birnau and Immenstaad. The lake stores warmth and in so doing creates a less variable climate and makes for a longer mild fall.

Two types of grapes define viticulture by the lake: the light grape of Müller-Thurgau for white wines with a flowery bouquet and the red grape of Spätburgunder (Pinot Noir) made into full-bodied red wine or into fruity pink "Weißherbst", typical of Lake Constance.

Another popular wine is the fragrant Bacchus as well as the Ruländer (Pinot Gris in a rich, sweetish style), which is increasingly being sold as a fully dry wine, labeled "Grauburgunder".

Top: The vineyard Haltnau by Meersburg has belonged to the Spitalkellerei Konstanz for almost 800 years

Middle and bottom: Grapes of the Müller-Thurgau and the Pinot Noir

p.50: In the Seepark of Hagnau stands a massive Torkel, a winepress from the year 1747

51

Hagnau

Hagnau is a small winegrowing and fishing village amid orchards and vineyards. Thanks to its central location by Lake Constance, numerous wine and village festivals, as well as vacation programs for children, Hagnau is a pleasant holiday resort.

In 1881 the pastor and author Heinrich Hansjakob founded the first Baden winegrower's association. It helped to

* Idyllic winegrowing and fishing village
* Well located cafes and restaurants, comfortable hotels, boardinghouses, and vacation homes
* Approximately 1,400 inhabitants
* Oldest Baden winegrower's association
* Natural beach, camping site
* Fruit and wine trails
* Shipping pier

improve the quality and profitability of winegrowing and to enforce reasonable prices for wine. Since 1993 the 129 winegrowers of the association refrain from using herbicides and insecticides. This is made evident by the systematic planting underneath the vines on the 130 hectares under cultivation.

Top: Town hall

Bottom: Monument to the pastor Hansjakob

p.52: Hagnau lies amid vineyards and orchards

Immenstaad

Immenstaad also has a long and varied history. The community ascribes the name "Immos Gestade" (Immo's shore) to its Alemannic founder Immo. The oldest preserved construction is the well-fortified tower of the parish church of St. Jodokus, which bears a sign inscribed with the year 1474. There are still some old farmhouses in the center, but the rapid growth of the community has changed its image. This growth is due to the arrival of the Dornier concern and the change from a winegrowing and fishing village to a holiday resort suited for families.

It offers a great variety of events for visitors and locals all through the year, and thanks to its central location it is an ideal starting point for excursions around the lake.

* Family-friendly holiday and recreational resort with several awards
* Industry on the eastern border (Dornier and others)
* Approximately 5,900 inhabitants
* Indoor pool "Aquastaad" with outdoor beach
* Shipping pier, round trips on the "Lädine", a historic freight sailing boat
* Sailing and windsurfing school, boat rental, 3 yacht harbors, camping sites
* First adventure high-wire park in Germany
* Skate park, tennis hall, playground etc.
* Apple trail and many more walks and trails

Top: Shipping pier

Middle: The Schwörerhaus from 1578 already survived the Thirty Years' War

Bottom: View from the shipping pier of the St. Jodokus church

p.54: Immenstaad with its shipping pier and marina. In the background to the right lies Helmsdorf Castle and another marina and behind these the Dornier company premises

Leisure Time
on the Lake

Already during Roman times ships sailed the lake to transport grain, wine, salt, building material, and travelers. In 1991 the wreck of an 18 meter long freight sailing boat from the fourteenth century was found off the banks of Immenstaad. It was conserved and is now being displayed in the Archaeological Regional Museum in Constance.

In the Late Middle Ages other freight ships, the "Lädinen", which were up to 30 meters long and rigged with yardarms, started replacing these freight sailing boats. The Lädinen, in turn, were replaced by motorized ships more than a hundred years ago. The Immenstaad Lädinen Association has reconstructed a 17 meter long Lädine, with which offers round trips of one or two hours for up to 45 persons. For people who do not sail themselves, this is the easiest way of gathering a first impression of sailing and of finding out more about the history of sailing on Lake Constance.

For experienced sailors and windsurfers the lake offers a wide spectrum of sailing, from calm weather sailing right up to serious challenges during stormy weather.

p.56: Strong winds lure windsurfers to the lake

Top left: Sailing at sunset

Top right: The Immenstaad Lädine

Middle: Stormy Lake Constance

Bottom: Sailing regatta

Friedrichshafen

In 1811 King Friedrich I. of Württemberg united the previously free city of the Empire of Buchhorn and the former monastery Hofen into one city, ordered the construction of a larger harbor, and gave the city his name. In the following years he had the monastery turned into a palace, which from 1828 to 1918 served as a summer residence for the kings of Württemberg and which nowadays is the residence of the Duke of Württemberg.

The "Schlosskirche" (Palace Church), which is connected to the palace, was built between 1695 and 1701 under Christian Thumb and is considered one of the most beautiful Baroque churches in Upper Swabia. The two 55 meter high onion towers are visible from far away. They are the landmarks of Friedrichshafen.

* Largest industrial city by Lake Constance
* Administrative center of the Lake Constance district since 1973
* Approximately 58,000 inhabitants
* Trade fair, airport, Zeppelin Hall, car ferry
* Graf Zeppelin Haus, Zeppelin Museum, School Museum
* Well-known landmark: the towers of the Baroque Schlosskirche
* Annual "Seehasenfest" and many more festivals

Top: View of the palace and the Schlosskirche

Bottom: Altar of the Schlosskirche

p.58: The onion towers of the Schlosskirche are the landmark of Friedrichshafen

Friedrichshafen

Bank Promenade and Museums

We take the ship to Friedrichshafen and go from the shipping pier over to the big white building of the former railroad harbor station, which since 1996 accommodates the Zeppelin Museum "Technology and Art". More than 2 million people have visited this, the world's largest museum on the technology and history of airships. In so doing, they have also visited the salons and passenger cabins of a 33 meter long reconstructed part of the airship LZ 129 Hindenburg.

Now we take a stroll along the bank promenade past various cafés, the gondola port, the city park, and the marina. This takes us to the "Graf Zeppelin Haus" (Count Zeppelin House), the primary cultural and congress center in Friedrichshafen. Close by is the School Museum, dedicated to the history of schools. Among other things it has classrooms authentically furnished as they were in times around 1850, 1900, and 1930.

Top left: Ice cream café by the bank promenade

Top right: Lookout tower by the pier

Middle: In the city park

Bottom: By the Uferstraße

p.60: Old town with the bank promenade, in front lie the gondola harbor and St. Nicholas Church, behind lies the ship and ferry harbor with the white building of the Zeppelin Museum

Friedrichshafen

The Trade Fair and Zeppelin City

The history of modern day industry in Friedrichshafen began when, at the end of the nineteenth century, Count Ferdinand von Zeppelin received a piece of land in Manzell from the King of Württemberg in order to build an airship yard. On July 2, 1900 the first navigable airship LZ1 took off for an evening flight from the bay right in front of the yard. It had a length of 128 meters and the flight ended 18 minutes later before Immenstaad.

Subsequently, the "Luftschiffmotorenbau GmbH" (airship motor factory, later Maybach, today MTU), the

"Zahnradfabrik Friedrichshafen" (gear factory, today ZF), the Dornier factory (today part of EADS), and the diversified Zeppelin Company were all set up here. After the end of the era of the 245 meter long large-sized zeppelins, it took 60 years until the first flight of a "New Technology" zeppelin in September 1997. Approximately 20,000 passengers a year can now enjoy the

view of Lake Constance and other regions of Germany and neighboring countries on round trips in the low-flying "Zeppelin NT".

Numerous hotels, the international airport, and the largest trade fair grounds in Baden-Württemberg all complete the infrastructure of the "Trade Fair and Zeppelin City" Friedrichshafen.

Top left: Round trips in the 75 meter long Zeppelin NT offer up to 13 passengers a birds-eye view of the sights around Lake Constance

Top middle: The fountain in front of the city hall symbolizes the products of Friedrichshafen's industry

Top right: Sailing boats on the trade fair lake during INTERBOOT, Friedrichshafen's largest trade fair

Middle: Monument to the Count in front of the Graf-Zeppelin-Haus

p.62: New Friedrichshafen trade fair grounds, in the foreground the Zeppelin hall

Traveling by Ship on Lake Constance

Modern navigation on Lake Constance began in 1824 when the steamship "Wilhelm" was put into operation in Friedrichshafen. It traveled the routes from here to Romanshorn and Rorschach. In 1847 Friedrichshafen became the first city around the lake to receive a railroad link. It was called the "Swabian Railroad", about which a popular song was made. In the following years many more railroad tracks followed, ending in Romanshorn, Lindau, and Constance. Seeing as there was no interconnected railroad system along the banks of the lake, a lively traffic of passenger ships evolved between these four cities. From 1869 onwards unmotorized freight barges, which would carry several railroad freight cars, were attached to the ships.

In 1928 the car ferry between Konstanz-Staad and Meersburg was put into operation. In 1929 the ferry between Friedrichshafen and Romanshorn followed, which carried railroad freight cars up until 1976. Apart from these two ferry lines and several thousand private boats, there are about 30 passenger ships of the "Weiße Flotte" (White Fleet), which travel to more than 40 destinations around Lake Constance. The largest of these ships can carry up to 1,200 passengers.

Top: The motorboat MS Karlsruhe, which has been in service since 1937, was renovated in 2004

Bottom: Säntis Mountain in the background

p.64: Ships of the White Fleet and the car ferry Euregia in the harbor of Friedrichshafen

Eriskirch

Eriskirch is a little village on the river Schussen, which flows down from Ravensburg. The village has been able to avoid the bustle of some other holiday resorts and offers a much more rural vacation closer to the farms. An old covered wooden bridge crosses the river Schussen. The Eriskirch Reed lies between the village and Lake Constance. This nature reserve has a width of about one kilometer and has expansive moor and reed areas. From the end of May the Siberian Iris starts to flower there.

Eriskirch's landmark is the Gothic Church of Mary with its pointed tower, which is visible from far away. The parish and pilgrimage church was built around the year 1400 and was partly renovated after the Thirty Years' War. The frescoes, which are now visible, the stained glass windows, and the Madonna have remained intact from the fifteenth century.

Top: The tower of the church Unsere Liebe Frau is visible from far away

Bottom left: Siberian Iris flower in the reed from the end of May

Bottom right: Sanctuary of the Marienkirche with old frescoes

p.66: A picturesque wooden bridge spans the river Schussen

67

Tettnang

The former district town of Tettnang lies amid orchards and hop plantations. The Counts of Montfort reigned here from the thirteenth to the eighteenth century. From 1712 to 1720 they built the magnificent New Palace on a hill. The extensive and lengthy restorations after a fire in the year 1753 put them so heavily into debt that the last of the Counts of Montfort had to hand over the palace to Austria.

* Former district town (until 1972) in the center of the fruit and hop cultivation area
* Until 1780 residence of the Counts of Montfort, after that Austrian, Bavarian, and Württembergian administrative center
* Approximately 18,000 inhabitants
* Hop Museum, Hop Trail, Palace Museum, Montfort Museum
* Various cultural events

The famous Tettnang hop is cultivated on an area of about 1,300 hectares. About 2,000 metric tons are exported each year to all parts of the world for the production of high-quality beer.

Apart from this, about 10,000 tons of fruit are produced, and asparagus from Tettnang is appreciated not only in the various hotels and restaurants of the city.

Top: The Torschloss and a restaurant that has gained fame through its asparagus specialities

Bottom: 2,000 tons of hop cones and 10,000 tons of fruit are sold annually

p.68: The magnificent New Palace from the eighteenth century towers above orchards and hop gardens

Langenargen

Langenargen is situated between the river mouths Schussen and Argen. Its landmark is the Montfort Palace, situated on a peninsula and visible from far away. This was the original site of the moated castle Argen of the Counts of Montfort. However, the line died out and the castle fell into disrepair. It was even plundered for building material. From 1861 King Wilhelm I. ordered the construction of the new palace in the then modern Moresque style on the site of the old castle.

Germany's oldest cable suspension bridge crosses the river Argen. It was built between 1896 and 1898 by Karl Leibbrand and has a span of 72 meters. As its designer was involved with the design and construction of the Golden Gate Bridge (1933 to 1937), a rumor was started which suggested that the Golden Gate Bridge was just an enlarged reproduction of this Swabian bridge, which is under monumental protection.

* Resort town close the Argen river mouth
* Approximately 7,000 inhabitants
* Montfort Palace with café, restaurant and disco
* Outdoor pool with beach, indoor pool, sports center
* State Institute for Lake Research
* Fish hatchery
* Art museum
* Annual "Match-Race" sailing regatta
* Diverse program of events

Top: The oldest cable suspension bridge in Germany spans the Argen River by Langenargen

Bottom: Resting by the lake banks

p.70: The holiday resort's landmark, Montfort Palace, is visible from far away

Wasserburg

The former fishing village on the Bavarian banks of Lake Constance has turned into a family-friendly, appealing climatic health resort. From far away we can already see the parish church St. Georg with its Baroque onion tower, as well as the old castle from the fourteenth century, on the picturesque peninsula.

Originally the peninsula was an island, and a drawbridge connected the castle with the mainland. When the bridge fell into disrepair in the eighteenth century, the owners of the castle could not afford a new bridge and so they had the channel between the island and the mainland filled. Nowadays, the castle serves as a hotel, and the peninsula has been equipped with a small harbor and a shipping pier.

Wasserburg is also the home of the author Horst Wolfram Geißler, whose novel "Der liebe Augustin" stands out as a monument to the Bavarian area of Lake Constance.

Top: The landmark of Wasserburg is the Baroque church of St. Georg

p.72: View of the picturesque peninsula

Lindau

Lindau is the southwesternmost city in the "Freistaat Bayern" (Free State of Bavaria) and is an important tourist center by Lake Constance. The core of Lindau is the island with its historic old town and the lake harbor.

* Largest Bavarian city by the lake
* Approximately 24,000 inhabitants
* Historic old town on the island with a surface area of 0.68 km²
* Well-known landmark: harbor entrance with the lighthouse and the Bavarian Lion
* Historic old city hall, numerous churches, and towers of the Middle Age city fortifications
* Theater, Opera of Marionettes, City Museum
* Congress center, casino
* Annual conference of Nobel Prize winners
* Fun pool "Limare", several outdoor pools, artificial ice rink

Lindau (= Linden-Island) is mentioned for the first time as the name of a convent in a document dating back to the year 882. In 1079 Lindau was granted the right to hold markets and in 1396 it became a free city of the Empire. The most notable event of the Late Middle Ages was the Imperial Diet in the old city hall. A band of frescoes on the southern facade of the city hall is a constant reminder of the arrival of the princes.

Top: Maximilian Street is the most beautiful shopping street on the island

Bottom: The band of frescoes on the old city hall portrays the arrival of Duke Philipp of Burgund, who represented his father Emperor Maximilian I.

p.74: The landmark of Lindau is the harbor and its entrance

Lindau

Old Town on the Island

The island is connected to the mainland via a road bridge and a railroad causeway. Between the two lies the "little lake", a popular place for ice-skating during cold winters. On the borders of the old town several towers of the medieval city fortifications have remained intact. The Diebsturm (thieves' tower) has an unusual shape considering the four oriels in its spire. The Peterskirche (St. Peter's church) is close by. It is Lindau's oldest church with mural paintings done by Hans Holbein the Elder.

The Protestant Stephanskirche (St. Stephen's Church) and the Catholic Stiftskirche (Minster) are situated close to each other. The older St. Stephen's Church was altered from 1780 onwards in the Baroque style. The

Minster of St. Mary was erected in the middle of the eighteenth century on the site of the Romanesque minster, which burnt down in 1728.

The most beautiful of all middle-class houses, the "Haus zum Cavazzen" is also situated on the market square. There are more richly painted middle-class houses dating back to the fifteenth to eighteenth century in the Maximilianstraße and the other streets of the pedestrian zone.

Bottom: Figures in fancy dress of Lindau's Fasnacht (carnival)

Top: The Diebsturm with its four pointed oriels is also called Malefizturm and served as the city prison during the Middle Ages

Middle: Cafés by the lake promenade

p.76: On the left side of the picture lies the lake promenade with the old lighthouse (Mangturm), in the background lie the Catholic Collegiate Church (gray spire) and the Protestant church St. Stephen (green spire)

Lindau

The Lake Harbor

The new lake harbor was completed in 1856. For many decades it connected the Bavarian railroad network with the other cities around Lake Constance. It was also an important harbor for the transfer of railroad freight cars onto freight barges that were attached to ships.

The harbor entrance with its 33 meter high lighthouse and the sitting Bavarian Lion on the opposite side has become the most well-known landmark of Lindau.

The Old Lighthouse (Mangturm) with its colorful roof tiles dates back to the thirteenth century and was part of the city fortifications during the Middle Ages. One can climb up both towers from where one has a marvelous view of the old town and Lake Constance.

Top: Lighthouse and Bavarian Lion have been welcoming arriving ships and boats since 1856

Bottom: Harbor entrance by night

p.78: Animated bank promenade with the Mangturm

79

Bregenz

In the year 15 B.C. Roman soldiers conquered the Celtic Brigantion and founded the trade and military base Brigantium. The medieval old town is today's Oberstadt (upper city) and has cobblestone streets, old churches, and the Martin's Tower, which is capped by a massive onion tower.

* Capital of the Austrian state of Vorarlberg since 1918
* Textile, food, and machine industry
* Approximately 28,000 inhabitants
* During Roman times important harbor city with the name Brigantium
* Well-known through the Bregenz Festival on the Floating Stage
* Vorarlberg State Museum, Art House, Casino
* Indoor lake pool, outdoor pool with beach

In 1523 Bregenz fell under the rule of the House of Habsburg and the center of the city steadily moved down from the upper city to the banks of the lake. This is where the Floating Stage of the world renowned Bregenz Festival (Bregenzer Festspiele) with its approximately 7,000 seats is situated. Every year, up to 200,000 spectators can watch the "Spiel auf dem See" (Play on the lake).

Top: The Floating Stage in the years 2003 and 2004 with the scenery for the musical "Westside Story"

Bottom: Martin's Tower was originally used as a storeroom and was converted to a watchtower in the year 1600

p.80: The old post office, built in the Viennese Ringstraße architectural style, and the modern art house, built in 1997, both as seen from the lake promenade

Pfänder
Mountain

Pfänder Mountain (1064 m) towers above Bregenz. A cabin funicular brings us from the city to the mountain peak in six minutes. At the top we are welcomed by a panorama restaurant, a marvelous view of Lake Constance, and an alpine game park.

While walking through this park we can observe deer, marmots, ibex, and other animals from the Alps in their natural environment. A particular attraction is the raptor show. In a demonstration lasting 40 minutes, different bird species fly in the upwind of the Pfänder slopes while their behavior and habits are explained in detail.

Pfänder Mountain with alpine game park and the Adlerwarte Pfänder towers above Bregenz

p.82: Large-size cabins of the panorama cable car lead up to the peak of the 1064 meter high Pfänder Mountain

Rhine Delta

From Pfänder Mountain we have a view across the Rhine Delta to the Swiss mountains. On the southwestern corner of Bregenz's city limits the Bregenzer Ach leads into the lake, as do the Dornbirner Ach and the channeled "New Rhine" behind the village Hard. The Rhine carries enormous amounts of sediments, which will have filled Lake Constance in about 15,000 years. The Rhine Delta is mostly unpopulated and serves as a biosphere for various aquatic birds.

The village Hard is where the last remaining paddle steamer on Lake Constance, the "Hohentwiel", is docked. She made her maiden voyage in 1913 and was taken out of service in November 1962. After a few years as a club house and some less than esthetic renovations the ship seemed destined to be scrapped. In order to save the steamer, the association "International Lake Constance Shipping Museum" was founded. The steamer was subsequently restored according to plans dating back to 1913. Since May 1990 the Hohentwiel is again traveling the lake and reminds us of the great era of steamships.

Top: The salon steamer SD Hohentwiel was built in the year 1913 and is the last preserved steamer on Lake Constance

Middle: Captain Kloser, the chief of the Hohentwiel for many years

Bottom: By the mouth of the Old Rhine

p.84: The mouth of the channeled New Rhine reaches far into the lake. To its right lies the alluvial plain of the Rhine Delta with the peninsulas Rohrspitz and Rheinspitz, behind which the mouth of the Old Rhine lies hidden

Altenrhein and Rorschach

The "Old Rhine" constitutes the border with Switzerland. Just across it lies the little village of Altenrhein with a regional airport and an aviation museum. Its most recent sight is the art and market hall, which was built according to a design by Friedensreich Hundertwasser.

Rorschach

* Only harbor town in the canton of St. Gallen
* Approximately 9,000 inhabitants
* Museum of Local History in the former granary, Veteran Car Museum in the "Alte Garage"
* "Badhütte Rorschach" and other pools
* Rack railway to Heiden with a modern railcar or with the "Nostalgia Steam Train"
* Lake and river boat trip to Rheineck
* Annual sand sculpture festival on the banks of the lake

Rorschach served as the harbor for the monastery of St. Gallen and in the year 947 it received the right to trade, mint coins, and levy import duties. The landmark of Rorschach is the Kornhaus by the harbor, which was built between 1746 and 1748. For a long time it served as a granary for wheat and other grains from Southern Germany, which were transported across Lake Constance on Lädines. In 1824 was the first time that a paddle steamer, laden with about 40 tons, made the trip from Friedrichshafen to Rorschach. In 1856 Rorschach was connected to the railroad network, and since 1875 there is a rack railway with which one can reach the Biedermeier village of Heiden, which lies 400 meters higher, in a trip of half an hour.

The rack railway to Heiden not only has modern railcars, it also has a nostalgia steam train with the locomotive Rosa and 5 open carriages

Top: Market hall of Altenrhein according to a design by Friedensreich Hundertwasser

Middle: The Kornhaus by the harbor is the landmark of Rorschach

p.86: View of the bay of Rorschach

Arbon

In the first century A.D. the Romans conquered the Celtic settlement Arbona. Around the year 280 they built the fort Arbor Felix on the strategically favorable spit. When Irish itinerant monks reached Arbon around the year 610, they found a Christian community which had remained intact since Roman times. The monk Gallus stayed and founded a hermitage further to the south, from which the monastery of St. Gallen came into being.

* Largest industrial city of the canton of Thurgau
* Approximately 13,000 inhabitants
* Old town with medieval buildings
* Museum of History in Arbon Castle, Veteran Car Museum, Juice and Distillery Museum
* More than 3 km of the lake banks equipped with parks, pools, harbors etc.

In the Middle Ages the city of Arbon fell into the possession of the prince bishops of Constance, who ordered the construction of the castle in 1515. The economic boom began in the seventeenth century with the fabrication of linen and the subsequent international linen trade. About a hundred years ago Arbon then became the center of the machine and textile industry of eastern Switzerland.

Top: View of the old Catholic church St. Martin from the Old Harbor

Bottom: Half-timbered house from the seventeenth century

p.88: The so-called Römerhof was a corner tower of the city walls from the thirteenth century

89

Romanshorn, St. Gallen and Säntis

With regard to traffic, Romanshorn is located in a very central position. With the construction of the largest harbor on Lake Constance (1841) and its connection to the railroad network (1855), the city evolved from a small fishing village to a major point for cargo handling. Its central location also makes Romanshorn an ideal starting point for excursions by bike, ship, train, or car around Lake Constance and to the Swiss foothills of the Alps.

Romanshorn

* Important junction and centrally located holiday resort
* Approximately 9,000 inhabitants
* Largest harbor on Lake Constance and home to the Swiss Lake Constance fleet
* Car ferry to and from Friedrichshafen
* Numerous recreational facilities

One of our destinations is St. Gallen with its Baroque cathedral and its world famous collegiate library.

Somewhat further is the 2,502 meter high Säntis Mountain. From the Schwägalp in the Appenzellerland we go by a modern, heated cable car (built in 2000) to the peak in just a few minutes where we are welcomed by a panorama restaurant and several terraces that offer a magnificent view. Since 1995 there is a 123 meter high needle-shaped radio tower on the peak, which on clear days can be seen from the northern banks of Lake Constance, more than 40 km away.

Top: Collegiate library and cathedral of the monastery of St. Gallen

Bottom: The car ferry Friedrichshafen, like the other ships of the Bodensee-Schiffsbetriebe (BSB), has belonged to the Stadtwerke Konstanz since the year 2003

p.90: On clear days one can see Säntis Mountain (2502 m) from the northern banks of Lake Constance, over 40 km away. In the front, by the lake is Romanshorn, behind it parts of the city of St. Gallen

Reichenau Island

Via Kreuzlingen we arrive back in Constance, from where we go along the Lake Rhine until we reach the Lower Lake. It makes up about an eighth of the total surface area of Lake Constance and is not as deep as the Upper Lake. In the middle of the Lower Lake lies Reichenau Island (= rich island). The island is known as one of the "cradles of occidental culture" and is famous for its three Romanesque churches and the cultivation of vegetables, both outdoor and in greenhouses. The UNESCO added Reichenau Island to its World Heritage List on November 30, 2000.

Since 1838 a two kilometer long causeway connects the island to the mainland. On it is an avenue which is lined with poplars. A statue of Bishop Pirmin awaits us by the side of the road. The bishop founded the first monastery on the island in 724 with forty monks. Some of the later abbots were chancellors, advisors, and educators for princes at the court of Emperor Charlemagne and his descendants.

* Island in the Lower Lake with a surface area of about 4.3 km²
* First monastery founded in 724 by the itinerant bishop Pirmin
* 3 community districts with 3 famous Romanesque churches
* Vegetable cultivation on 2.4 km² of which 0.5 km² in greenhouses
* Annual harvest of over 18,000 tons of fresh vegetables
* Wine-growing on about 0.2 km²
* Since 1838 connected to the mainland via a causeway
* Numerous hotels, boarding houses, and holiday homes

Top: Reichenau and the Gnadensee, as seen from the Swiss banks of the lake

Middle: Bishop Pirmin by the side of Pappel Avenue

Bottom: Vegetable cultivation

p.92: Reichenau Island is situated in the middle of the Lower Lake

Reichenau Island

Three Roman-esque Churches

The three Romanesque churches originate from the ninth to the eleventh century, when the monastery with its notable library and its schools strongly influenced occidental culture.

The Minster of St. Maria and Markus in Mittelzell is the former monastery church. It was enlarged several times, but its oldest part was already consecrated in 816. An opulent treasure chamber also belongs to the minster. Since 1991 it also has a herb garden, which was laid out according to a didactic poem written by the abbot Strabo almost 1200 years ago.

The column basilica, St. Georg, with its three naves is situated in Oberzell and

dates back to about the year 900. It is famous for its mural paintings from the tenth century. The pictures represent the miracles of Christ and are considered the culmination of the Reichenau School of Painting.

St. Peter and Paul in Niederzell was built around the year 1100. The most valuable work of art in this church is the mural in the eastern apse, which shows Christ as the Pantocrator (ruler of all) over the apostles and the prophets. It was painted around 1110.

Romanesque churches (top left St. Georg and top right St. Peter and Paul) and vegetable cultivation characterize Reichenau Island

Top middle: Christ as the ruler of all in the eastern apse of St. Peter and Paul

Middle: The mural paintings in St. Georg portray the miracles of Christ

p.94: The Minster of St. Maria and Markus was enlarged several times in the course of the centuries. In front is a herb garden in medieval fashion

The Lower Lake and Allensbach

The Lower Lake around Reichenau Island is bordered by three mountain ranges: the Bodanrück to the north, the Swiss Seerücken to the south, and the Schiener Berg with the peninsula Höri to the west. The part of the lake to the north of Reichenau is called Gnadensee (Mercy Lake), and the part south of Radolfzell and the peninsula Mettnau is called Zeller See.

The Lower Lake
* Part of Lake Constance with approximately 70 km²
* Of these, about 10 km² shallow water designated nature reserve
* Greatest depth 46 meters
* Cities on the German banks: Allensbach with the world renowned Allensbach Institute for Demoscopy, Radolfzell, Moos, Gaienhofen with the Hermann Hesse Museum, Hemmenhofen with the Otto Dix House
* Cities on the Swiss banks: Ermatingen, Mannenbach, Berlingen, Steckborn

Large parts of the areas around the banks are wetlands or flood plains. The Wollmating Reed, which covers an area of almost 8 km², and other areas have been designated nature reserves.

About 300 bird species have been sighted there and about 600 plant species have been found.

Directly opposite Reichenau Island, on the northern banks of the Gnadensee, lies Allensbach, world renowned for the "Allensbach Institute for Demoscopy", which was founded in 1947.

Top left: The main building of the Institute for Demoscopy (opinion research) is a former farmhouse from the seventeenth century

Top right: The center of Allensbach

Bottom: The convent of Hegne of the Merciful Sisters of the Holy Cross also belongs to Allensbach

p.96: View from Allensbach across the Gnadensee to Reichenau Island

Radolfzell

adolfzell is the largest city by the Lower Lake and owes its name to Bishop Radolf from Verona, who, in the year 826, ordered the construction of a few houses and a church here, in the immediate proximity of Reichenau Abbey. Apart from the

* Largest city on the Lower Lake
* Approximately 29,000 inhabitants
* Car-free old town, lake promenade, museums, and cultural center
* Peninsula Mettnau with cultural center "Healing through Movement" and 1,4 km² nature reserve
* Various sports and leisure time facilities
* Annual "Hausherrenfest" and water procession in Moos

Top: On the Mettnau peninsula

Middle: The former city moat nowadays is a well-kept park

p.98: The Late Gothic minster with its 82 meter high spire, which was only built in 1903, is the center of the old town

Marcus Relics for the minster on Reichenau, around the year 830 he also brought the relics of two Saints of Asia Minor, Theopontus and Senesius. In the eleventh century a relic of St. Zeno from Verona was added. With these three "Hausherren" (town patron saints), who were represented and honored in a similar way to the

Three Kings, Radolfzell became an important place of pilgrimage.

Radolfzell received a city charter in 1267 and belonged to the House of Habsburg from 1298 to 1805. When the city was connected to the railroad network the settlement of industry led to the growth up to its current size.

Singen am Hohentwiel

To the west of Radolfzell (and therefore no longer directly by Lake Constance) lies the Hegau landscape with its numerous cone-shaped hills, which are extinct volcanoes. The most well-known of these is Hohentwiel (689 m) with the largest castle ruins in Germany. This is where in 914 Swabian noblemen founded a castle, which for a long time seemed impregnable and withstood all attacks during the Thirty Years' War. On May 1, 1800 the castle had to be handed over to Napoleon's army and was subsequently destroyed. The "romantic" ruins were rediscovered for tourism in the late nineteenth century.

View of Hohenstoffeln Mountain (844 m) across ruins

p.100: The shadow of our Zeppelin is passing Hohentwiel Mountain. Behind it lies the industrial city of Singen

* Modern industrial and shopping city
* Approximately 45,000 inhabitants
* Several large industries
* Museums, art hall, theater, cultural center
* Annual Hohentwiel Festival with music and variety shows in the castle ruins

The city of Singen had already been mentioned in documents dating back to the year 787. It could, however, never develop as it was always overshadowed by the mighty Hohentwiel Castle. It was only after the town had been developed as a railroad junction and after the first large industries had settled here (Maggi 1887) that Singen was declared a city in 1899.

The Höri Peninsula

To the south of Singen the Schiener Berg rises to about 300 meters above the level of the lake. The mountain itself and the areas where it descends to the banks make up the Höri Peninsula. The small rural villages of the Höri Peninsula were combined to form three communities with about 3,000 inhabitants each: Moos to the north, Gaienhofen in the middle, and Öhningen to the southwest. Each village is surrounded by fields and orchards. Areas around the banks between the villages that are not being cultivated have been declared nature reserves.

The idyllic location of Höri and its former seclusion attracted a number of artists. The most well-known among these were Hermann Hesse, who lived in Gaienhofen for a few years, and Otto Dix, who settled down in Hemmenhofen. Museums have been dedicated to each of these artists. Even in modern times several artists still live on Höri. This is why the communities of Höri can offer their modern day guests and visitors a multifaceted art and literature program, with drawing courses, poetry readings, and literary trails.

Top: Sunset with a view of Höri

Bottom left: Half-timbered houses in Horn

Bottom middle: Hermann Hesse Museum in Gaienhofen

Bottom right: The old fishing house in Wangen nowadays accommodates the Museum of Local History

p.102: The Lower Lake by Iznang

Switzerland by the Lower Lake

The villages Ermatingen, Mannenbach, Berlingen, and Steckborn on the southern banks of the Lower Lake were in the possession of Reichenau Abbey for several centuries. They only became part of the Swiss canton Thurgau in 1798. Until today, Ermatingen and Berlingen have remained fishing villages with beautiful half-timbered houses and good fish restaurants.

Mannenbach is especially famous for the Napoleon Museum in Arenenberg Castle in the district of Salenstein, which is situated further up the slopes. The small castle was the residence of Napoleon's stepdaughter Hortense, mother of the Emperor Napoleon III., who spent his school holidays and parts of his student years here. From the terrace of the estate we have a splendid view of the Lower Lake.

In Steckborn several of the medieval buildings of the old town center have been preserved. The town's landmark is the "Turmhof", built in 1320, which nowadays houses a museum.

View from the terrace of Arenenberg Castle in the direction of Berlingen

In the Napoleon Museum

Left: The city hall of Steckborn was built in 1669

Arenenberg Castle

p.104: Directly by the banks of the lake lies the small Turmhof Castle

Stein am Rhein

By Stein am Rhein the Lower Lake narrows to reform the Rhine River. In the second century the Romans already built a bridge over the river here. The village of Stein am Rhein was mentioned for the first time in a document from the year 1001 and has an old town center with picturesque houses dating back to the sixteenth and seventeenth century.

Especially the town hall and the numerous restaurants around the originally preserved market square have magnificently painted facades. Other worthwhile buildings are the Romanesque city church from the twelfth century, the former monastery St. Georgen, and the medieval city fortifications.

High above Stein am Rhein and a few vineyards for the "Steiner Beerli" lies the entirely preserved castle Hohenklingen from the eleventh century. Nowadays the castle is a popular destination for trips. From the "Bergfried", from the "Laube", or from the windows of the restaurant one can enjoy the view of the picturesque city of Stein am Rhein as well as the landscape around the Lower Lake and the Rhine River.

Top: From Hohenklingen Castle one has a beautiful view of the Rhine Valley

Bottom left: The focus of the market square is the picturesque city hall

Bottom right: Stein am Rhein with the pointed spire of the Romanesque city church

p.106: By Stein am Rhein the Lower Lake narrows to form the Rhine River

Schaffhausen

I n 1045 Schaffhausen received the right to mint coins. For a long time it was a free city of the Empire and was accepted into the "Bund der Eidgenossen" (Swiss Confederation) in 1501. The middle-class houses in the old town, which are decorated with oriels, remind us of these days. The spire of the Romanesque minster from the twelfth century and the tower of the Gothic parish church of St. Johann look out above the old town.

* Capital of the canton Schaffhausen
* Approximately 34,000 inhabitants
* Well preserved, car-free old town
* Theater, cultural center, concerts, and festivals
* "Museum zu Allerheiligen" (Museum of the All Saints Monastery), Halls for Modern Art und more museums
* Numerous festivals and markets

The landmark of Schaffhausen, Fort Munot, lies above the city. It was built from 1564 to 1589 as a circular bastion, apparently according to an idea by Albrecht Dürer, who in 1527 wrote about the advantages of circular fortifications. Nowadays, the southern slopes are used for the cultivation of the Pinot Noir vines of Schaffhausen.

Top: View from Fort Munot up the Rhine River

Left: Central tower of Fort Munot

p.108: Fort Munot towers above the houses of Schaffhausen

Rhine Falls

* Largest waterfall in Europe
* Height of the falls: 23 meters
* Width of the falls: 150 meters
* Average amount of water during summer: 600 m³/s
* Average amount of water during winter: 250 m³/s
* 1965 and 1999 records with over 1200 m³/s
* Approximately 2 million visitors annually
* Annual "giant fireworks" on 1st of August, the Swiss National Holiday

The Rhine Falls by Schaffhausen (in the village Neuhausen) is the largest waterfall in Europe and offers us a grand spectacle at the close of our round trip. Across a width of 150 m and a height of 23 m about 600 cubic meters of water per second pass over the rocks during the summer months.

Below Neuhausen short paths lead from the parking lot to the 13 meter deep Rhine Falls basin. Here we find several restaurants and kiosks as well as the riverside castle "Wörth". From here we can admire the might of the water masses, or we can take a small boat to the middle rock of the falls and climb up it.

The southern half of the Rhine Falls (from the middle rock) belongs to the canton of Zürich. On the southern banks a footpath leads down from Laufen Castle to the lookout points Fischetz and Känzeli as well as to a landing stage.

Top left: One can reach the middle rock of the Rhine Falls with a boat

Top right: The Rhine Falls in the summer

p.110: The Rhine Falls with a railroad bridge and Laufen Castle

Imprint

Publishing and distribution:
Stadler Verlagsgesellschaft mbH, 2004
Max-Stromeyer-Straße 172
78467 Konstanz

© Copyright by
Verlag Friedr. Stadler, Konstanz
Inh. Michael Stadler

Layout and typesetting: Olaf Zeidler, Konstanz

Translation: Eldad Louw, Freiburg

Printed in Germany

German edition
"Am Bodensee"
ISBN 3-7977-0504-2

English edition
ISBN 3-7977-0507-7

Photography:
All pictures by Dr. Rolf Zimmermann except:
p.19 top and p. 65 top, Stadtwerke Konstanz GmbH;
p.25 middle, Mainau GmbH, picture archives;
p.37 bottom, Markgräflich Badische
Hauptverwaltung, Schloss Salem;
p.83 bottom Pfänderbahn AG/D, Walser

Front endpaper: Extract from the
"Schwabenkarte" (Swabian map)
"Totius Sveviae novissima tabula" by
Janssonius, Amsterdam 1633

Back endpaper: Foehn storm in the fall

The Publisher wants to thank the following companies for their support.
They will be happy to supply you with further information related to the Lake of Constance.

Bodensee-Schiffsbetriebe GmbH
Hafenstraße 6
D-78462 Konstanz
Phone +49(0)75 31/36 40-389
Telefax +49(0)75 31/36 40-373
e-mail info@bsb-online.com
Internet www.bsb-online.com

Stadtwerke Konstanz GmbH
Max-Stromeyer-Straße 21–29
D-78467 Konstanz
Phone +49(0)75 31/803-0
Telefax +49(0)75 31/803-123
e-mail info@stadtwerke.konstanz.de
Internet www.sw.konstanz.de

DORNIER

Lindauer DORNIER GmbH
Rickenbacher Straße 119
D-88129 Lindau/Germany
e-mail webmaster@lindauer-dornier.com
Internet www.lindauer-dornier.com

Meersburg Tourismus
Kirchstraße 4
D-88709 Meersburg
Phone +49(0)75 32/440 40-0
Telefax +49(0)75 32/440 40-40
e-mail info@meersburg.de
Internet www.meersburg.de

Tourist-Information Friedrichshafen
Bahnhofplatz 2
D-88045 Friedrichshafen
Phone +49(0)75 41/30 01-0
Telefax +49(0)75 41/725 88
e-mail tourist-info@friedrichshafen.de
Internet www.friedrichshafen.de

Verkehrsverein e.V. Lindau
Ludwigstraße 68
D-88131 Lindau (B)
Phone +49(0)83 82/26 00 30
Telefax +49(0)83 82/26 00 26
e-mail info@lindau-tourismus.de
Internet www.lindau-tourismus.de

Pfahlbaumuseum Unteruhldingen
Strandpromenade 6
D-88690 Uhldingen-Mühlhofen
Phone +49(0)75 56/85 43
Telefax +49(0)75 56/58 86
e-mail info@pfahlbauten.de
Internet www.pfahlbauten.de

HAGNAUER
Wein vom Bodensee

WINZERVEREIN HAGNAU AM BODENSEE
Strandbadstraße 7
D-88709 Hagnau
Phone +49(0)75 32/10 30
Telefax +49(0)75 32/13 42
e-mail info@hagnauer.de
Internet www.hagnauer.de

Stadtmarketing Konstanz GmbH
Obere Laube 71
D-78462 Konstanz
Phone +49(0)75 31/28 24 80
Telefax +49(0)75 31/282 48 11
e-mail schaal@stadtmarketing.konstanz.de
Internet www.stadtmarketing.konstanz.de

Spitalkellerei Konstanz
Brückengasse 16
D-78462 Konstanz
Phone +49(0)75 31/128 76-0
Telefax +49(0)75 31/128 76-11
e-mail info@spitalkellerei-konstanz.de
Internet www.spitalkellerei-konstanz.de

Zeppelin Museum Friedrichshafen
Seestraße 22
D-88045 Friedrichshafen/Germany
Phone +49(0)75 41/38 01-0
Telefax +49(0)75 41/38 01-81
e-mail info@zeppelin-museum.de
Internet www.zeppelin-museum.de

Mainau GmbH
D-78465 Insel Mainau
Phone +49(0)75 31/303-0
Telefax +49(0)75 31/303-248
e-mail info@mainau.de
Internet www.mainau.de